my BIG BOOK of Numbers

Written by Karen Wane

Numbers are fun!

BRIMAX

For Raf, Barnaby and Maisie ~ K.W.

Illustrated by Mary Lonsdale

First published in Great Britain in 2001 by Brimax
An imprint of Octopus Publishing Group Ltd
2–4 Heron Quays, London, E14 4JP
© Octopus Publishing Group Limited

Mary Lonsdale courtesy of SGA

Created by Derek Hall and Associates
Designed by Kit Johnson

Printed in China

ISBN 1 8585 4317 7

Check your answers at the back.

Contents

Numbers and Counting 6

Adding Up 8

Taking Away 10

The Ten Family 12

Bigger Numbers 14

Having a Guess 16

Odds and Evens 18

Jumping Numbers 20

Which Goes First? 22

Parts of Numbers 24

More Adding Up 26

Doubling 28

The Difference Between 30

Multiplying 32

More Multiplying 34

Dividing 36

More Dividing 38

Measuring and Comparing 40

More Measuring 42

Organising Information 44

Answers 46

Numbers and Counting

1 One **2** Two **3** Three **4** Four **5** Five

Counting. We use counting to tell us how many things there are. We count using numbers. The more things there are, the bigger the number. We can write numbers in words or in numerals, like we have at the top of the page.

I'm clever, I can count up to ten. Can you?

Yes, and I can count backwards, too!

Look at this desert island. See if you can count…

1 palm tree   2 clouds   3 turtles   4 dolphins   5 seagulls

6 crabs   7 seashells   8 seahorses   9 starfish   10 fish

6 Six · 7 Seven · 8 Eight · 9 Nine · 10 Ten

How many spots are there on each mug?

Enough for everyone? These three turtles are having breakfast. Lots of other things in this picture are also in groups of three. Can you count them all?

It's time to do the washing up! Can you count all the bowls? How many are there?

Throw me one!

Adding Up

Three and one hop is four.

1   2   3   4   5

0
Zero

I'm one elephant.

Adding together.
When we add two numbers together, we get a new number.

And I'm one elephant.

A new number.
Zero is a number, too. Zero is also called nought. Zero stands for "nothing". When zero is added to a number, that number doesn't get any bigger – because "nothing" has been added to it.

1 elephant

What's one add one?

1 elephant

A bigger number.
Now we've added the elephants together, we have made a bigger number.

1 elephant and 1 elephant makes 2 elephants

This is like one and one and one!

Adding another.
Now we've added another elephant, we have an even bigger number.

1 elephant and 2 elephants makes 3 elephants

A plus sign shows we are adding things together.
This means add.

An equals sign means **the same as**, or **makes**.
This means equals.

Seven and three is ten.

6   7   8   9   10

Hopping along. Use the lily pads to help you add up. Put your finger on the number you want to add to. Now hop with your finger, from pad to pad. Each hop adds on one. Count the hops as you go. The number you land on is the answer.

Climb aboard!

3 + 0 + 2 = 5

See how many children are going for a ride on the elephant, by adding them up. First there are three children. At the next stop, no one gets on, so there are still three. Next, two more children get on. Add these to the three already on board, and it makes five!

Can you add together these things in the picture?

1 palm tree + 2 palm trees =

1 ball + 2 balls + 3 balls =

3 dragonflies + 5 dragonflies =

1 sun + 0 sun =

4 sunshades + 2 sunshades =

1 frog + 3 frogs + 4 frogs =

There's more adding on page 26.

Taking Away

We're ten budgies...

I've taken one coconut away.

So that leaves two coconuts.

I've got four coconuts.

Getting smaller. When we take away, the new number we get is always smaller than the number with which we started.

If the baby monkey takes one coconut away, how many will be left?

Taking away. Here are the elephants we added together on page 8. Now we are going to take one away.

Remember, two plus one equals three.

3 elephants

In other words. Taking away is also called **subtracting**.

Taking away...

...is the opposite of adding up!

3 elephants take away 1 elephant leaves 2 elephant

A minus sign shows we are taking something away.

This means minus.

Flying away. What number do we get when three budgies fly away from a group of ten? Check the budgies have got the answer right by holding up your ten fingers. Now put three fingers down, to show the three birds flying away, and count how many fingers are left.

5 – 0 – 2 = 3

The children are on their way back home now. There are five children on board the elephant. At the first stop, no one gets off, so there are still five. At the next stop, two children get off. Take these away from the five still on board, and that leaves three!

Look at these two pictures. Lots of things have been taken away in the right-hand picture. Can you see what's missing and finish the sums?

3 monkeys – 2 monkeys =

5 butterflies – 3 butterflies =

7 flowers – 5 flowers =

4 stars – 0 stars =

6 bracelets – 1 bracelet =

1 moon – 0 moons =

11

The Ten Family

10
Ten

A very useful number. Ten is a very special number. When you first learned to count, you started by counting to ten.

These are the number pairs that make ten.

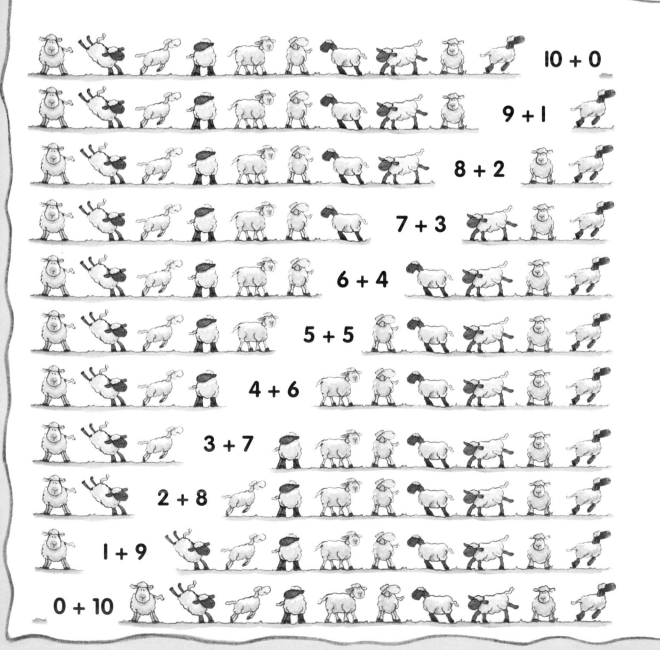

10 + 0

9 + 1

8 + 2

7 + 3

6 + 4

5 + 5

4 + 6

3 + 7

2 + 8

1 + 9

0 + 10

Making ten. New numbers are made by adding smaller numbers together. On the left are the ways you can make ten, using different number pairs. See if you can learn these number pairs by heart.

More hopping. The lamb and the chicken are counting how many more hops they need to get to ten. We can do this for other numbers, too. You can use your fingers or toes to help you - you've got ten of each!

In this farm picture, there are ten different animals in each field, but some are sheltering from the rain. Can you work out how many of each type of animal are sheltering, by counting the ones still outside?

Bigger Numbers

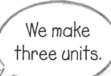

We make three units.

More than ten. When we want to count a large number of things, we can first partition them into groups of ten. We call these **tens**. The things left over are called **units.** Then we add together the tens, and next we add on the units.

This is called a 100 square.

How many geese? Let's count the geese at the top of these pages. There are two groups of ten geese (making twenty), and three geese (making three units) left over. So we add up the number like this:

10 + 10 = 20

20 + 3 = 23 **geese.**

Here are lots of eggs. Count the tens and units, and add them up, to see how many there are.

We use just nine numbers and zero to make all other numbers.

ten unit	ten unit	ten unit	ten unit	ten unit	ten unit	ten unit	ten unit	ten unit	ten unit
1	2	3	4	5	6	7	8	9	10
11	12	13	14	15	16	17	18	19	20
21	22	23	24	25	26	27	28	29	30
31	32	33	34	35	36	37	38	39	40
41	42	43	44	45	46	47	48	49	50
51	52	53	54	55	56	57	58	59	60
61	62	63	64	65	66	67	68	69	70
71	72	73	74	75	76	77	78	79	80
81	82	83	84	85	86	87	88	89	90
91	92	93	94	95	96	97	98	99	100

A 100 square has ten rows, with ten numbers in each row.

Picking apples. The apples are going to be picked. There's room for ten apples in each box, but there may be some left over. How many are left?

Loads of apples. Now the full boxes are loaded onto the truck. Count the number of boxes. How many apples are there on the truck?

More apples! This big lorry is waiting for the small truck to arrive. How many boxes are already on board? And how many apples?

Even more apples! The boxes on the truck are loaded onto the big lorry, and off it goes to market. How many boxes are there altogether now? And how many apples?

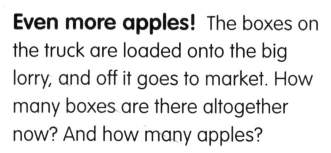

Having a Guess

I just can't count all those balloons.

Why do we guess?
Sometimes we guess, or **estimate**, a number, because there isn't time to count properly, or because the number is too big to work out easily.

Well, have a guess!

Are there eighteen sweets?

Or twenty-four?

Or three

How many sweets in the jar? Have a guess, too, and then count the sweets to check whose guess is the closest.

I think I've got enough money for the rides.

Look at the picture, and have a guess! How many flags are there? How many coconuts? How many goldfish in the bowls on the hoopla stall? And how many hoops?

In other words. There are lots of words that mean the same as guessing. We could say **roughly**, **about**, **approximately** or **nearly**.

Sometimes we estimate whether there is enough to go round. Look at the picture…
Are there enough roundabout horses for everyone in the queue to get a ride?
Each seat on the Big Wheel has room for two. Will everyone get on?

Odds and Evens

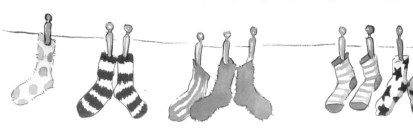

Even numbers. Look at these groups of socks on the washing line. In some of the groups, all the socks make matching pairs. There are no socks left over. These groups have an **even** number of socks.

> You can't put odd numbers of things in pairs.

> We're two. We're a pair... we're even!

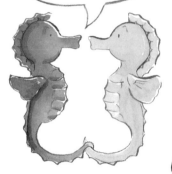

Odd numbers. In some of the other groups on the washing line, one sock is left over. These groups have an **odd** number of socks.

> I'm one. Am I odd or even?

Everyone needs a partner to join in the dance. Try putting the different kinds of animals into pairs. Is there an even number of starfish? Will they each have a partner? Is there an odd number of crabs? Will any be left over? Is there an even number of dolphins? Will each have a partner?

What will the next odd number be?

Will eight be odd or even?

A number pattern. Odd and even numbers form a pattern. One is an odd number, two is an even number, three is an odd number, but four is even. Can you see the pattern?

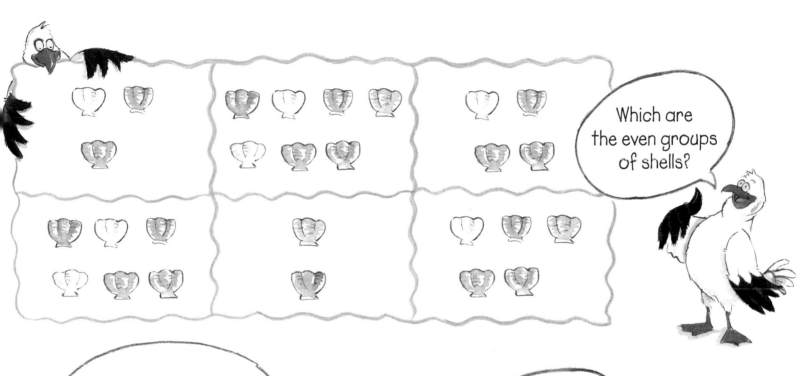

Which are the even groups of shells?

You need an even number of slices of bread to make a sandwich.

Whoops! Now there's an odd cup left over!

That's odd!

One cup and one saucer together make a pair. There was a cup on each saucer, but now there is one cup left over.

Jumping Numbers

More number patterns. We saw on page 19 how odd and even numbers make a pattern. There are lots of other patterns around us. Every third cactus above has a red flower. This time the pattern has changed from **every other** number to **every third** number.

There are lots of other sorts of patterns in this picture. How many can you see? Look around your home and see if you can find patterns on things like carpets, curtains, plates and even clothes.

My rug is red, yellow, red, yellow...

Nice striped pattern!

Number sequences. Turn back to page 14, and lay some tracing paper over the **100 square**. Now go to **square 5** and shade it in. Then jump to **every fifth square**, and shade them all in. Can you see the pattern? Now make a pattern by shading in **every fourth square**.

Hidden treasure. To find the buried treasure in the desert, go to Start and follow this number sequence: first go **down two** squares, then go **along three** squares, go **down two** more squares, **along three** squares, and **down two** squares. That's the spot!

Mind the cactus! Now find a number sequence that takes you from Start to the treasure square, but this time without landing on a cactus.

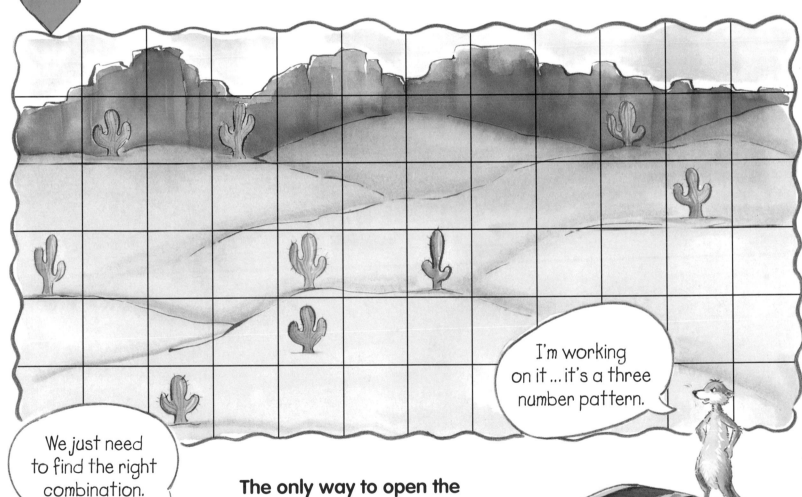

We just need to find the right combination.

I'm working on it...it's a three number pattern.

The only way to open the padlock on the treasure chest is to find the right combination. Work out the number pattern to find the last number:

7 6 5 7 6 5 7 6 ?

Which Goes First?

Wait for me – I'm last!

Number order. When we count numbers, like one, two, three and so on, we are putting them in order of size. We know that one is **smaller** than two, but that three is **bigger** than two. This is called **comparing** the numbers.

As we count from one...

...the numbers get bigger and bigger!

More or less? If we compare the number of bananas the big and small monkey have each got, we see that the big monkey has **more** bananas than the small monkey – or we could say the small monkey has **less** bananas than the big monkey.

You've got more bananas.

You've got less bananas.

Equal. The baby monkeys have one banana each, so they each have an **equal** number.

You've both got the same.

22

In order. We use numbers to put things like days of the month in order. Can you think of other things we put in order?

The animals are running a race. Who came first? (We can also write this as 1st.) Who came second? (We can also write this as 2nd.) Who came third? (We can also write this as 3rd.) We have used numbers to put the winners in order.

Numbers are useful!
We can use numbers to tell each other things.

Parts of Numbers

Equal parts. Numbers and other things can be divided into parts. If we divide something into two equal parts, each part is called a **half**. If we divide each half in half again, we will have four equal parts, each called a **quarter**. Another name for a part of a whole is a **fraction**.

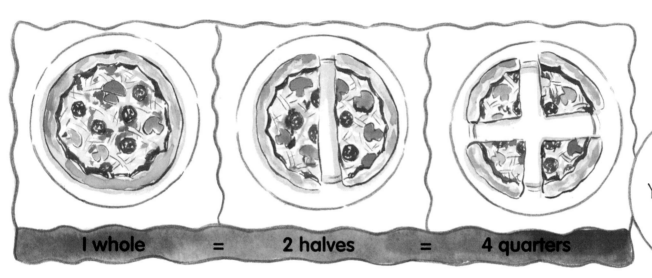

1 whole = **2 halves** = **4 quarters**

You're small! You've only got a quarter of a pizza.

Let's share! If you have a whole pizza, and a friend comes to tea, you can cut the pizza into two halves. If two more friends arrive, there will be four of you, and you can cut each half of the pizza in half again, to make four quarters – enough for everyone!

There are two of us mice.

Let's have half the sweets each.

How many make a half? Groups of things can be divided into fractions, too. Can you work out how many each mouse will get if they divide the sweets in half?

A quarter is a half of a half.

Four out of one!
If you have four presents to tie up, and one long piece of ribbon, you can cut the ribbon into four quarters – one for each present.

But I've only got half a glass left.

I've got a whole glass of juice.

Look at the party food in the picture. Which pie has only half left? How many parts is the birthday cake divided into? What fraction of the swiss roll has cherries? If the sandwiches are divided into two halves, how many in each half?

25

More Adding Up

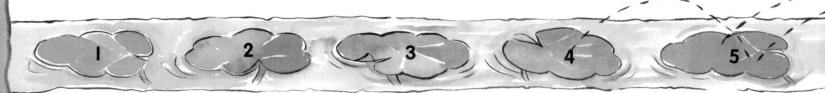

Any order. When you add numbers together, it doesn't matter which number goes first – the answer is still the same. Try this out by hopping your finger along the lily pads. First, start on number 4, and hop from pad to pad until you reach number 9. It's five hops, so you've added up like this: **4 + 5 = 9**. Now start on 5. It's four hops to reach 9, so: **5 + 4 = 9**.

That's one way to do it.

The order doesn't matter, even when you add together more than two numbers.

This monkey has six oranges, and two bowls. He's put two oranges in one bowl, and four oranges in the other bowl. We could write this as: 2 + 4 = 6. How many other ways could he put all the oranges into two bowls? (Use both bowls.) Can you write the answers as adding up sums?

Now how many different ways can the monkey put all the oranges into three bowls? (Again, using all three bowls.) Write the answers as adding up sums again.

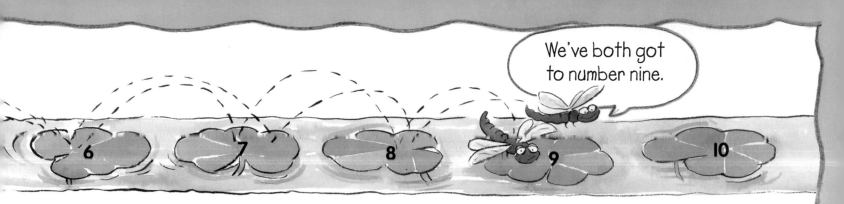

The monkey below is showing the children how to add up. But someone has rubbed off the numbers in some of the sums. What are the missing numbers?

Setting out sums. Sometimes when we're adding, we write the numbers underneath each other. So **6 + 3 = 9** can be written as:

$$\begin{array}{r} 6 \\ + 3 \\ \hline 9 \end{array}$$

What numbers complete the sums?

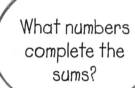

7 +   = 9

5 +   = 8

4 +   + 1 = 10

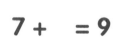

Adding bigger numbers.

It helps to write numbers one under the other when we are adding numbers bigger than nine. Then we can often turn a difficult sum into two easy ones! How would you add up **14 + 23**? First set the sum out like this:

Go back to page 14 for tens and units.

tens	units
1	4
+ 2	3
3	7

Now we add the **units** together. Then we add the **tens** together.
4 units + 3 units = 7 units (or 7),
1 ten + 2 tens = 3 tens (or 30),
3 tens + 7 units = 37
So the answer is thirty seven.

Doubling

Two of them. When we see something reflected, it's as if we see two instead of just one. It appears to have doubled.

Doubling numbers. We can double a number, too, by adding the same number to it. So, to double one, we add one to it. Double one makes two.

Doubling is the opposite of halving.

And halving is the opposite of doubling!

To find the double of all the numbers on the right, count the spots on both wings of each ladybird. Some of the doubles have already been worked out for you. Can you do the rest?

Finding the doubles of numbers up to ten

Double 1 is 2

Double 6 is ?

Double 2 is 4

Double 7 is 14

Double 3 is ?

Double 8 is ?

Double 4 is ?

Double 9 is ?

Double 5 is 10

Double 10 is ?

I think I'm seeing double!

What's next?

In each of the rows below, the second and third numbers are double the number before. What number comes next in each row?

1 2 4 ?

3 6 12 ?

5 10 20 ?

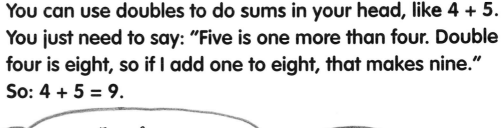

I've got double the number of legs you've got!

And I've got double the number of legs you've got!

You can use doubles to do sums in your head, like 4 + 5. You just need to say: "Five is one more than four. Double four is eight, so if I add one to eight, that makes nine." So: 4 + 5 = 9.

Doubling something makes it twice as big.

Four frogs add four frogs makes eight frogs.

And one more makes nine!

Do these sums by doubling and then adding one:
3 + 4 =   5 + 6 =   6 + 7 =   8 + 9 =

The Difference Between

We're both the same.

What's the difference? One useful way of comparing things is to see what is different about them. This is called the **difference**.

Look at our legs – we're different. Different is the opposite of the same.

Lots of legs! One big difference between an octopus and a starfish is the number of legs! Which has more? Let's find out by drawing their legs in boxes.

The octopus has eight legs.

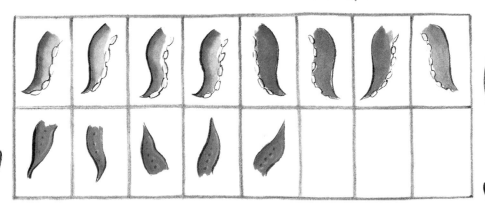

But the starfish only has five legs.

Comparing the rows of legs shows us that the octopus has three more legs than the starfish. You can only match five legs from each animal. So the difference between the number of legs is three. We can also write this as a take away sum: octopus's legs minus starfish's legs equals three. Or we could write: **8 − 5 = 3.**

6   7   8   9   10

Count the hops to find the difference.

On the hop! Another way to find the difference between two numbers is to count the number of hops **between** the numbers. Find the difference between 2 and 5 by hopping with your finger. Start with your finger on wave number 2. Hop from wave to wave until you reach number 5. Did you count three hops? That's the difference!

Look at this picture. What is the difference between the number of: Stripes on the blue fish? Fins on the pink fish? Spots on the seashells? Strands on the red and the green seaweed? Babies with each grown-up seahorse?

Drawing in boxes can help you work out the difference.

Multiplying

Numbers in sets. Many things come in groups or sets. A bicycle has a set of two wheels. To find the total number of wheels on several bicycles, we count the sets and add them together. If we do this, we are adding the same number over and over again. For six bicycles, we need to find the total of six sets of two. We would do the sum like this:
2 + 2 + 2 + 2 + 2 + 2 = 12.

In other words.
We can also say:
6 sets of 2 makes 12, or
6 lots of 2 makes 12, or
6 times 2 makes 12, or
6 multiplied by 2 makes 12.
This is called **multiplying**.
We write it like this:
6 × 2 = 12.

How many wheels?

My tricycle has three wheels, and so has yours.

So how many wheels is that?

3 wheels   ×   2   =   6 wheels

A multiplication sign shows we are multiplying numbers together.

This means multiply.

start

Try counting in sets.

Two sets of four wheels makes eight.

Multiplying by dots. You can use rows of dots to help you multiply. Let's multiply four by two again. Draw two rows, with four dots in each row. Two rows of four dots makes eight dots!

● ● ● ●
● ● ● ●

What do four rows of two dots make?

Turn the page to see the answer!

Each of the three boats below has one rower. The rowers will all want a drink after the race. To find the number of drinks needed, add three sets with one rower in each, like this: 1 + 1 + 1 = 3, or you could say: 1 x 3 = 3. So the answer is 3 drinks! In the next race, each boat has four rowers. How many drinks will be needed this time?

One times three is three times one!

Finish

33

More Multiplying

How many balls?

Let's multiply them.

Multiplying makes things easy! On the last page, we found that when we have sets of things to add up, like these balls, it's easier to do a multiplying sum instead of adding up the same number over and over again. There are special tables to help us do this!

2 Times Table				
1	x 2	=	2
2	x 2	=	4
3	x 2	=	6
4	x 2	=	8
5	x 2	=	10
6	x 2	=	12
7	x 2	=	14
8	x 2	=	16
9	x 2	=	18
10	x 2	=	20

Times tables. We so often do a multiplying sum that it's useful to know the answer to all the multiply or "times" sums, up to 10 times 10. To help us, there are Times Tables that we can learn. Start with the "2 Times Table".

Saying the Times Tables out loud makes it easier to learn them by heart.

You can multiply by two with this table.

Sports Day. Everyone wants to join in the team sports. But they need to know how many can take part in each event. The Times Tables can help us work this out!

The Doubles Tennis Tournament has six teams, with two players in each team. How many people can play in the Tournament? This sum is: 6 teams x 2 players, or 6 x 2.

34

That sounds hard!

Not if you learn your Times Tables!

5 Times Table

1	× 5	=	5
2	× 5	=	10
3	× 5	=	15
4	× 5	=	20
5	× 5	=	25
6	× 5	=	30
7	× 5	=	35
8	× 5	=	40
9	× 5	=	45
10	× 5	=	50

You can multiply by five with this table.

The Five-a-side Soccer Tournament has four teams. How many people can play altogether? This sum is: 4 teams x 5 players, or 4 x 5.

10 Times Table

1	× 10	=	10
2	× 10	=	20
3	× 10	=	30
4	× 10	=	40
5	× 10	=	50
6	× 10	=	60
7	× 10	=	70
8	× 10	=	80
9	× 10	=	90
10	× 10	=	100

You can multiply by ten with this table.

There are three Tug-of-war teams, with ten people in each team. How many people can join in altogether? This sum is: 3 teams x 10 players, or 3 x 10.

Five kittens and five presents...

Dividing

...that means there's one present each!

Sharing out. Dividing is another way of saying that you are sharing out something.

Half each! Dividing one thing between two is the same as halving it.

Dividing larger numbers. To divide four balloons between two friends, give one balloon to the first friend, one to the second friend, another to the first friend, another to the second friend… and then you have no balloons left!

| 4 to share out | I each, 2 left | I more each, none left |

Dividing four balloons between two friends is the same as finding out how many times we can take two away from four. We can do it twice, like this: 4 − 2 = 2, 2 − 2 = 0.

Four divided by two is two.

More people? If more than two people want to share something, it works just the same! If you want to divide six mince pies among three people, it's the same as taking three away from six twice: $6 - 3 = 3$, $3 - 3 = 0$.

Do you think we'll get more than one necklace each?

Will I get three crackers?

There's something for everyone at the party. If we divide the necklaces between the girls, how many will each one get? If we divide the crackers between the boys, how many will each one get? If we divide the balls between the kittens, how many will each one get?

More Dividing

There are nine of us kittens.

A **division sign** shows that we are dividing numbers. ÷

This *means* divide.

Dividing into groups. Sometimes we want to put things into groups, with the same number of things in each group. We can use dividing to help us work out how to do this.

The nine kittens want to play "piggy in the middle", so they must divide into groups, with three kittens in each group. How many groups will there be?

9 – 3 leaves 6 kittens on the bench

6 – 3 leaves 3 kittens on the bench

You can work out the number of groups by counting how many times you can take three away from nine:

9 – 3 = 6
6 – 3 = 3
3 – 3 = 0

Or you can write the sum more simply by using the division sign: 9 ÷ 3 = 3.

3 – 3 leaves 0 kittens on the bench!

38

Something left over. What happens when we divide three crusts among two robins? What can we do with the leftover crust? We can still divide it between the two robins. Do you remember how we do that?

Multiplying is the opposite of dividing. This is useful to know. Look at this picture of a Christmas decoration…

Each of these three empty boxes held four balls. To find the total number of balls, multiply the number of boxes by the number of balls in each box, like this: 3 x 4 = 12.

Now it's time to put the balls away! To find how many boxes we need, divide the total number of balls by the number of balls that will fit in each box, like this: 12 ÷ 4 = 3.

Measuring and Comparing

Why do we measure? We measure things to find out their size. Measuring also tells us what one object is like compared with another. Whenever we decide that one object is a different size from another, we are making a **comparison**.

You're very short.

And you're very tall.

It's easy to compare the giraffe and the porcupine. Can you compare the other things in the picture? Which is the highest bird? Which is the tallest mountain? Which is the thickest tree trunk? Which is the widest river?

The animals are off to the river, but the wall is in the way. Who'll choose the tall door? Who'll choose the wide door? Who is short enough to go through any of the doors?

Who fits the bed? Sometimes there's no need to measure. We can tell just by looking. We can see that only one of these birds will fit the small bed.

How long is long? These monkeys are using leaves to measure. By counting the leaves they can tell each other how long their snakes are.

More Measuring

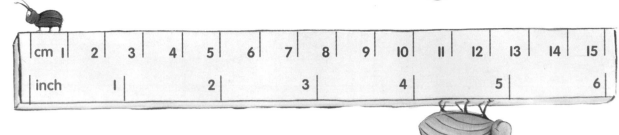

Easier than leaves! On page 41 the monkeys were using leaves to measure the snakes. To make it easier when we measure things, instead of leaves we use **standard units**, which are the same for people all around the world.

In some countries, the standard unit for length is a **centimetre**.

Cm is short for centimetre.

In other countries, the standard unit for length is an **inch**.

In is short for inch.

Your own ruler. Rulers and tape measures have the standard units marked on them to help us measure things easily. Trace the ruler at the top of the page. Now you have your own ruler!

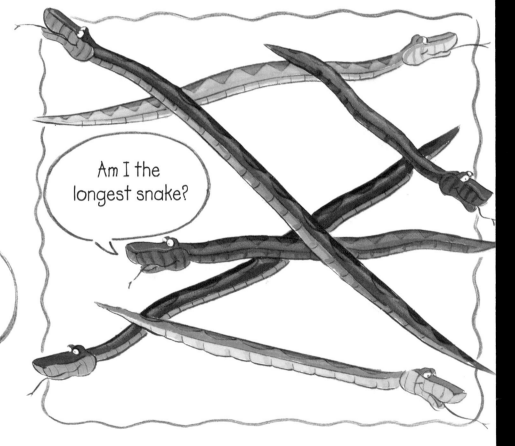

Am I the longest snake?

I'm measuring my hand with a ruler to see how wide it is. Can you measure yours?

Measure these snakes with your ruler to find out which is longest. How long is the green snake? Are both purple snakes the same length?

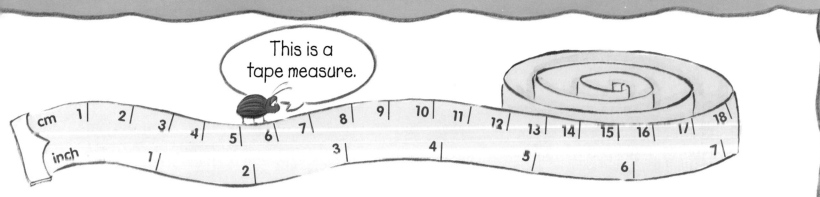

This is a tape measure.

Measuring big things! When we need to measure big things, we can use a tape measure. This has lots more centimetres or inches on it than a ruler.

One hundred centimetres is one metre.

Twelve inches is one foot.

Bigger units. To make it easier to measure very big things, standard units can be grouped into bigger units.

Measuring both ways. Rectangular objects have two different sides to measure. The longer measurement is called the **length**, and the shorter measurement is called the **width**.

I can swim a length!

But I can only swim a width!

Try this! Use a tape measure to measure some of the things in your home. For example, you could measure your bed to find out the **length** and the **width**.

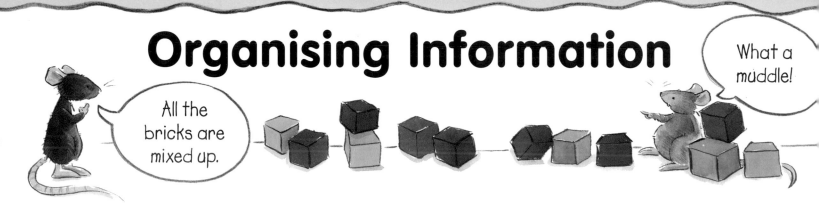

Organising Information

What a muddle!

All the bricks are mixed up.

Sorting things out. It's easier to understand things if we sort them out, or **organise** them. The bricks at the top of the page are all muddled up, so it's hard to see how many of each sort there are. The rats are organising them into groups to help us work it out!

Charts are useful! We can make **charts** to help us organise information.

Ben and Emma are feeling left out because they haven't got a pet. They think all their friends have pets, but they need to show their parents that it's true.

All our friends have pets.

If our parents knew that, maybe we'd get one, too.

Show them – make a chart!

Ben and Emma ask their friends what pets they have. Then they make a chart, like this:

	Jim	Alice	Paul	Sarah	Tom	Katie
Dog	✓		✓	✓		✓
Cat	✓	✓	✓	✓	✓	✓
Rat	✓				✓	

Each tick on the chart means the friend has a pet!

Can you answer these questions by looking at the chart?
How many friends did Ben and Emma ask about their pets?
Were Ben and Emma right – do all their friends have pets?
Which is the most popular pet? Which is the least popular?

Let's sort them out.

Now we can see what we've got!

The most popular pet! Ben and Emma have used the information from their first chart to make two more charts, to show the most popular pet. The chart on the right is a **bar chart**. It has a bar for each kind of pet...

Cats are most popular!

Dog   Cat   Rat

It even looks like a pie!

...and the one on the left is a **pie chart**. It's a circle, divided into twelve parts, because the friends have twelve pets altogether.

This is called a key.

■ Dog ■ Cat ■ Rat

Look at this picture of a pet shop. Make a bar chart and a pie chart to show how many animals of each kind there are.

45

Answers

Page 7

Spots on mugs 4, 2, 6, 3.

Things in threes Saucepans, cups, plates, tumblers, legs on stools, legs on table.

Bowls 8.

Page 9

Beach picture 3 palm trees, 6 balls, 8 dragonflies, 1 sun, 6 sunshades, 8 frogs.

Page 10

Monkey taking coconuts 3 left.

Page 11

Flying away 7 left.

Two pictures 1 monkey, 2 butterflies, 2 flowers, 4 stars, 5 bracelets, 1 moon.

Page 13

Farm picture 4 sheep, 7 cows, 8 horses, 1 pig, 5 hens, 0 ducks.

Page 14

Eggs 15.

Page 15

Picking apples 4 left.

Loads of apples 2 boxes, 20 apples.

More apples! 8 boxes, 80 apples.

Even more apples! 10 boxes, 100 apples.

Page 16

Sweets 14 (the closest guess was 18).

Flags 26 altogether.

Coconuts 22

Goldfish 13.

Hoops 13.

Page 17

Enough roundabout horses No.

Room on the Big Wheel Yes.

Page 18

Even number of starfish No.

Will each have a partner No.

Odd number of crabs No.

Will any be left over No.

Even number of dolphins Yes.

Will each have a partner Yes.

Page 19

Even groups of shells 4, 6, 2.

Page 21

Hidden treasure The square with the treasure is marked with an X.

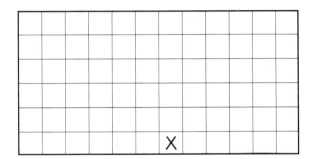

Mind the cactus Go down three, along three, down three, along three.

Combination 765765765.

Page 22

In order Some things we put in order would include: hours in a day, pages in a book, houses in a street.

Page 23

Race Ostrich 1st, hippo 2nd, giraffe 3rd.